MENUS from the CUPBOARD

MENUS *from the* CUPBOARD

Charlotte Coleman-Smith

LifeStyle

With thanks to family and friends
for their ideas and encouragement.
And to James, with love.

Recipes by Charlotte Coleman-Smith
Photography by Tine Drost

This edition first published in Great Britain in 1999 by
LifeStyle
An imprint of Parkgate Books
Kiln House, 210 New Kings Road, London SW6 4NZ

© 1999 Parkgate Books

A CIP catalogue record for this book is available from the British Library.

ISBN 1-902617-04-5

Printed and bound in Hong Kong

Contents

Contents continued

Introduction

What do you cook if friends drop in unexpectedly? As long as you've got pasta, some pesto or tins of tomatoes, some dried herbs and garlic, you can always knock up a passable pasta dish – add a glass of wine or two and no-one will be complaining. However, if this is what you would normally cook for yourself, and in order for life not to be one long round of pasta and tomatoes, it is good to be able to expand your repertoire – with the minimum of effort, of course. All you need is a certain amount of backup in your fridge, freezer, larder and cupboard. It's not difficult to call in just a few more items so that your day-to-day cooking is more adventurous. Once you get used to cooking with a wider variety of ingredients you will automatically keep them stocked up every time you go shopping. Eventually you'll always have a broader base to cook from.

All the recipes in this book are fairly simple and very adaptable. Salads, bakes, pasta and rice dishes are perfect ways to experiment and use up leftovers or store cupboard staples. Use what you have, experiment with different types of vegetables, different types of beans, of pasta, rice and flavourings and think laterally. If you don't have vinegar, use lemon juice, and vice versa, and if you've no fresh tomatoes use a tin. Instead of sausages try using bacon – and the type of cheese used in a bake or a gratin can also be varied. Try Parmesan instead of Cheddar, or breadcrumbs and a little butter for a crunchy topping if you've no cheese. Instead of making a rich white sauce as a base for a meat dish or casserole, use condensed mushroom or chicken soup.

In the spirit of this book, I have not included a huge number of recipes for cuts of meat or fish as such things should be bought fresh when they're needed. This doesn't mean that the store cupboard cook has to be vegetarian, but it does mean that other ingredients get more of a look-in.

A wok is a great asset – you'll often need fresh veg as the main ingredient in a stir-fry, but you can try an infinitesimal number of combinations using store cupboard ingredients, as long as they are interestingly spiced and flavoured. As you'll see in the stir-fry chapter, garlic, ginger and spring onions are essential for lifting a dish above the ordinary.

MENUS FROM THE CUPBOARD is for anyone who works, gets home late and wants to eat interestingly and well without having to leave the house to go shopping again. In other words, it's for most people who have a life outside the kitchen!

THE REC

The Basics

Aim to have at least some of the following items always to hand:

Cupboard
- A good stock of tins: butter beans, kidney beans, chickpeas, tuna, sardines, anchovies, chopped tomatoes, spinach, sweetcorn, condensed soup

- Dried food: rice, pasta, noodles, couscous, lentils

- Nuts and dried fruit: pine nuts, almonds, walnuts, sesame seeds, raisins

- Condiments: olive oil, sunflower oil, wine vinegar, balsamic vinegar, tomato sauce, dried spices and herbs, stock cubes, mustard, soy sauce, jams, honey, chutneys, salt and black pepper, sugar, flour, tomato purée, garlic purée, 'lazy ginger', sherry or cooking wine

Larder
spring onions, salad leaves, garlic, onions, tomatoes, red or green peppers, potatoes, lemons or limes, fresh bread

Fridge
butter, milk, cream, eggs, Greek yogurt, bacon, sausages, Parmesan cheese, fresh herbs, pesto sauce, tomato sauce, ready-washed salad leaves

Freezer
peas, fish fillets or steaks, mince, red berries, pastry, stock, ice cream, extra bread

DIPS

AND PATÉS

These are the ultimate in fast first courses – all you need are some tins, one or two fresh ingredients and a fork or food processor. Serve them with brown bread or toast as a starter, or with soup for a light meal.

Guacamole

This can be served as a first course with a platter of raw vegetables such as carrots, radishes and tomatoes (i.e. crudités), or as a dip with corn chips.

Peel, stone and mash the avocados in a bowl. Add the lime juice and stir gently. Add the remaining ingredients and mix. Chill for 30 minutes (you can place an avocado stone in the mixture to prevent discolouration). Sprinkle with paprika before serving.

To prepare: 5 minutes

To chill: 30 minutes

SERVES
4-6

INGREDIENTS

2 large ripe avocados

2-3 tbsp lime juice

200g/7oz chopped tinned tomatoes, drained

1 garlic clove, crushed

pinch of hot chilli powder

pinch of ground cumin

2 tsp clear honey

small bunch fresh coriander, finely chopped

salt and freshly ground black pepper

TO SERVE

crudités or corn chips, and a sprinkling of paprika

Houmous

To prepare: 15 minutes

Houmous is so easy to make that you will wonder why you ever bothered to buy it from a shop. You can buy tahini from most large supermarkets and healthfood stores. This recipe is quite garlicky, but you can vary the quantities of lemon and garlic according to taste. If you're unsure, be conservative – you can always add more and whizz it all up again.

In a food processor, whizz the chickpeas, tahini, lemon juice, garlic and olive oil until smooth (if you want a coarse spread, mash the ingredients together with a fork). Add more lemon juice and garlic according to taste. Turn into a bowl and sprinkle with paprika. Serve with pitta bread, warmed in the toaster.

INGREDIENTS

1 x 420g/15oz tin chickpeas, drained

3 level tbsp tahini (sesame seed paste)

juice of ½ lemon

1 or 2 garlic cloves, crushed

3 tbsp olive oil

TO SERVE

warm pitta bread, cut into strips and a sprinkling of paprika

Mixed Fish Pâté

You can use frozen prawns here, but make sure they are thoroughly defrosted.

Open the tins of salmon and tuna, reserving the juices and oil from each tin. Remove any dark skin from the salmon. Flake the fish in a bowl together with the oil. Place the breadcrumbs in another bowl with the melted butter, lemon juice and rind. Add the flaked fish and prawns, stir in the anchovy essence, then the cream, and season to taste. Turn into a serving dish or individual ramekins. Chill for 1 hour if possible. Serve with brown bread and lemon wedges.

To prepare: 15 minutes

To chill: 1 hour

INGREDIENTS

1 x 185g/6½oz tin salmon (in oil)

1 x 185g/6½oz tin tuna (in oil)

170g/6oz fresh white breadcrumbs

110g/4oz butter, melted

juice and freshly grated rind of 2 lemons

110g/4oz cooked peeled prawns, roughly chopped

3 tsp anchovy essence

285ml/½ pint single cream

salt and freshly ground black pepper

TO SERVE

brown bread and lemon wedges

SERVES 6-8

Mushroom Pâté

Wipe the mushrooms then trim them and chop very finely. Melt the butter in a frying pan and add the onion. Cook until softened – about 5 minutes. Add the garlic and mushrooms and continue to cook gently until the mushrooms are soft and any liquid has evaporated. This will take 15-20 minutes. Stir in the vinegar, dried herbs, and season to taste with salt and pepper. Remove from the heat and leave to cool. Put the cottage cheese into a bowl, add the mushroom mixture and stir to blend. If you want a smooth pâté, blend in a food processor. Spoon into a serving dish or individual ramekins, cover and chill for 1 hour if possible. Serve with warm French bread.

To prepare: 30 minutes

To chill: 1 hour

INGREDIENTS

900g/2lb open cup mushrooms

30g/1oz butter

1 medium onion, finely chopped

2-3 garlic cloves, finely chopped

1 tbsp balsamic vinegar

dried herbs (e.g. thyme)

salt and freshly ground black pepper

230g/8oz cottage cheese

TO SERVE

French bread, warmed

Smoked Mackerel Pâté

Bring the butter and cream cheese to room temperature. Skin the mackerel fillets and flake the flesh. In a bowl, cream the butter then beat in the cream cheese. Add the flaked fish, lemon juice, horseradish sauce, salt, pepper and cream. Mash together with a fork, or transfer to a food processor and blend to a smooth paste. Serve with thin slices of toasted brown bread and lemon wedges.

To prepare: 15 minutes

INGREDIENTS

55g/2oz butter

110g/4oz cream cheese

225g/8oz smoked mackerel, or 2 medium fillets

juice of ½ lemon

2 level tsp horseradish sauce

salt and freshly ground black pepper

4 tbsp single cream

TO SERVE

toasted brown bread, lemon wedges

and a sprig of dill

Tuna Pâté

This is very simple and surprisingly good. If you are in a huge rush, leave out the chilling time – the pâté will be slightly runny but just as delicious.

Mash the tuna with a fork, then add the butter and mix well. Alternatively, combine the tuna and butter in a food processor. Add the lemon juice and seasoning to taste. Turn into a serving dish or individual ramekins. Chill for 1 hour if possible. Serve with brown bread and wedges of lemon.

To prepare: 10 minutes

To chill: 1 hour

INGREDIENTS

1 x 185g/6½oz tin tuna

110g/4oz fresh butter, at room temperature

juice of 1 lemon

salt and freshly ground black pepper

TO SERVE

brown bread, lemon wedges

Tzatziki

Peel the cucumber, cut it in half lengthways and scoop out the seeds with a teaspoon. Cut the cucumber lengthways into thin strips and across into fine dice. Place the diced cucumber in a colander and sprinkle with salt. Allow to stand for 30 minutes, then rinse in cold water and dry well with kitchen paper. Mash the garlic to a purée with a little salt. Turn the yogurt into a mixing bowl and add the garlic, diced cucumber, olive oil, wine vinegar, a seasoning of pepper and the mint. Stir to blend and taste for seasoning. Turn into a serving bowl and chill for 1 hour if possible. Serve with strips of warm pitta bread.

To prepare: 45 minutes

To chill: 1 hour

INGREDIENTS

½ cucumber

salt and freshly ground black pepper

1 garlic clove

450g/1lb Greek-style yogurt

2 tbsp olive oil

1 tsp white wine vinegar

2 tsp chopped fresh mint (or ½ tsp dried mint)

TO SERVE

pitta bread, warmed and cut into strips

SOUPs

Although you can buy very good ready-made soups in the supermarkets, they are really so easy and satisfying to make that it's worth the extra effort.

If you have time and some spare bread – it can be a little stale – make some croûtons for sprinkling over the top of soups. They're also very good for adding texture to salads.

Remove the crusts from some thickly sliced white bread and cut into cubes. Melt some butter in a frying pan and sauté the cubes until golden. To make garlic croutons, fry the bread with a little crushed garlic.

CROUTONS

Broccoli Soup

In a large pan, bring the chicken stock to the boil and add the broccoli pieces. Cook, covered, for about 15 minutes or until the broccoli is tender. Purée the mixture in a food processor then stir in the cream. Season to taste with salt and pepper and the lemon juice.

To prepare: 5 minutes

To cook: 20 minutes

INGREDIENTS

855ml/1½ pints chicken stock

450g/1lb broccoli florets, cut into small pieces

2 tbsp double cream

salt and freshly ground black pepper

juice of ½ lemon

TO SERVE

a sprinkling of lightly toasted sesame seeds (optional)

Butter Bean and Pasta Soup

This soup is very filling and can be served as a light lunch or supper with some bread and a salad.

In a large pan, heat the olive oil and gently fry the onion with the garlic for about 10 minutes. Add the tomato purée and basil, stir for 1 minute, then add the butter beans and water. Bring the soup to simmering point and simmer gently for 5 minutes. Season to taste with salt and pepper. Blend the soup in a processor or blender (or push it through a sieve) to make a smooth purée, then return to the pan and add the macaroni. Cook gently for a further 10 minutes, stirring occasionally, then serve with the Parmesan.

To prepare: 10 minutes

To cook: 30 minutes

INGREDIENTS

2 tbsp olive oil

1 large onion, finely diced

2 garlic cloves, crushed

2½ tbsp tomato purée

1 tsp dried basil

1 x 400g/14oz tin butter beans, drained

855ml/1½ pints water

110g/4oz macaroni

salt and freshly ground black pepper

TO SERVE

50-75g/ 2-2½oz freshly grated Parmesan

Carrot and Coriander Soup

You can replace the carrots with other root vegetables, or use different herbs if you wish to experiment or if you don't have the exact ingredients listed here.

Heat the butter in a large pan, add the onion, cover the pan and cook over a low heat for 5 minutes. Add the carrots, potatoes and ground coriander, stir well, cover the pan and cook gently for 10 minutes, stirring from time to time. Add the stock or water, bring to the boil, then simmer gently for about 15 minutes, until the carrots are tender. Pour the soup into a blender or food processor and blend until smooth. Return to the pan and thin with a little water if necessary. Reheat the soup and season to taste. Stir in the cream (or pour the soup into bowls and use the cream as a garnish). Snip the coriander leaves over the soup before serving.

To prepare: 10 minutes

To cook: 30 minutes

INGREDIENTS

30g/1oz butter

1 onion, finely diced

450g/1lb carrots, peeled and sliced

230g/8oz potatoes, peeled and diced

1 tsp ground coriander

855ml/1½ pints vegetable stock or water

salt and freshly ground black pepper

140ml/5fl oz single cream (optional)

TO SERVE

fresh coriander leaves

Chilled Cucumber Soup

This is an elegant dish, and perfect for a summer's evening or a light lunch. Chill it for as long as you can to bring out the flavours.

Put the cucumber chunks into a food processor with the onion, garlic and a third of the yogurt. Blend until smooth, then add the rest of the yogurt and the cream, if using, and blend again. Add the vinegar and season to taste, then chill the soup in the refrigerator for as long as you can to allow the flavours to combine. Check the seasoning, then serve in chilled bowls.

To prepare: 10 minutes

To chill: 1 hour

INGREDIENTS

1 large cucumber, peeled and cut into chunks

1 small onion, finely diced

1 garlic clove, crushed

425ml/15fl oz natural yogurt

2-3 tbsp double cream (optional)

1 tbsp red wine vinegar

salt and freshly ground black pepper

TO SERVE

scatter with 1-2 tbsp chopped fresh chives or mint, or finely sliced cucumber

Mushroom Soup

Wipe the mushrooms, then chop them finely. Heat the butter in a large pan with the lemon juice and 2 tbsp water. When the mixture boils, add the mushrooms and garlic and stir to coat the mushrooms in the liquid. Cook gently for 3 or 4 minutes. Season with salt, pepper and the chopped fresh mint. Allow to cool a little, purée the mushrooms and liquid in a food processor, then return to the saucepan. Heat the cream in a separate pan, add to the mushrooms and stir to combine. Heat the stock, then add this to the soup with the wine. Simmer gently for 5 minutes. Serve hot.

To prepare: 10 minutes

To cook: 15-20 minutes

INGREDIENTS

200g/7oz flat cap mushrooms

30g/1oz butter

juice of ½ lemon

1 garlic clove, crushed

salt and freshly ground black pepper

2 tbsp fresh mint, chopped

55ml/2fl oz double cream

710ml/1¼ pints chicken stock

140ml/5fl oz dry white wine

SERVES 4

Pea and Lettuce Soup

This soup is quick to make and delicious served either hot or chilled.

Melt the butter in a large pan and add the peas, spring onions and lettuce. Cover and cook gently for 10 minutes, being careful not to brown the vegetables. Add the stock, mint, salt, pepper and sugar and cook until the peas are tender. Sieve or liquidize the soup until quite smooth. Swirl a tbsp of double cream over each serving and sprinkle with chives, if liked.

To prepare: 5 minutes

To cook: 15 minutes

INGREDIENTS

55g/2oz butter

450g/1lb frozen peas

110g/4oz spring onions, chopped

½ lettuce, washed and sliced

855ml/1½ pints chicken or vegetable stock

4-6 mint leaves

salt and freshly ground black pepper

1 level tsp sugar

TO SERVE

double cream, chives (optional)

Tomato Soup

This is an extremely quick store cupboard staple. If you have any fresh basil, chop it up and sprinkle it over the top to serve. If you don't have a potato, substitute with 2 tbsp plain flour, add this to the tomatoes and cook through for 5 minutes before adding the stock.

Heat the oil in a large saucepan, add the onion and potato and cook slowly for 10-15 minutes. Add the tomatoes and tomato purée and cook for 1 minute. Then add the garlic, basil and stock, season well, cover and simmer for 10-15 minutes. When the soup is ready, pass it through a sieve or whizz it briefly in a food processor. Check the seasoning. Serve with fresh bread or toast.

To prepare: 5 minutes

To cook: 30 minutes

INGREDIENTS

1½ tbsp olive oil

1 medium onion, chopped

1 medium potato, chopped

1 garlic clove, crushed

2 x 420g/15oz tins chopped tomatoes

1 tsp tomato purée

1 tsp dried basil

570ml/1 pint chicken or vegetable stock

salt and freshly ground black pepper

TO SERVE

fresh basil or parsley (optional), toast

SERVES 4

Watercress Soup

To prepare: 5 minutes

To cook: 40-45 minutes

To chill: 3 hours

A fresh-tasting peppery soup with a very pretty, delicate green colour. If you're watching your weight, leave out the cream. This soup is delicious served cold – chill for up to 3 hours and check the seasoning before serving.

Melt the butter in a saucepan, add the diced onion, the potatoes and watercress. Cover the pan and cook for 5 minutes, stirring now and then. Add the flour and seasoning and when the flour has cooked through (about 5 minutes), add the stock. Stir as it comes to the boil and simmer for 30 minutes. Strain the soup and serve in warm bowls, adding a swirl of double cream to each bowl.

INGREDIENTS

55g/2oz butter

1 onion, finely diced

450g/1lb new potatoes, peeled and sliced

1 bunch watercress, finely chopped

2 tbsp flour

salt and freshly ground black pepper

855ml/1½ pints vegetable stock

TO SERVE

double cream

SALADS

Salads make delicious main meals. Serve them with warm, crusty bread and perhaps a soup to start with. As side salads, they can play second fiddle to a main dish of poached chicken breasts, a plate of good, spicy salami, or a creamy quiche.

BASIC GREEN SALAD

For a very simple green salad, just mix a bag of salad leaves with some chopped herbs and sprinkle with olive oil, sea salt and a little lemon juice. This kind of salad is perfect eaten with cheese, cold meats, bread and a glass of wine. For more texture, add some croûtons (see page 18) and sprinkle over some cheese, bacon bits, nuts or chopped ham.

BASIC TOMATO SALAD

If you have some good, full-flavoured ripe tomatoes, make a simple salad by slicing them up, tearing over some shreds of fresh basil and drizzling over a little balsamic vinegar. Cherry tomatoes are very good for this. If you have any onions, or, even better, shallots, chop them up very finely and sprinkle over the tomatoes before adding the vinegar. You could also add some toasted pine nuts and slices of mozzarella cheese.

Dressings

Any basic salad can be livened up with a good dressing.

1. Vinaigrette

Mix the oil, vinegar and mustard together in a small bowl until smooth. Season to taste with pepper and a little salt.

Variation: use balsamic vinegar or lemon juice in place of the white wine vinegar.

INGREDIENTS

5 tbsp extra virgin olive oil

1 tbsp white wine vinegar

1 tsp mustard

salt and freshly ground black pepper

2. Honey and Soy Vinaigrette

Mix the oil, soy sauce, honey and mustard together in a small bowl until smooth. Season to taste with pepper and a little salt.

INGREDIENTS

5 tbsp extra virgin olive oil

1 tbsp soy sauce

1 tbsp honey

1 tsp mustard

salt and freshly ground black pepper

3. Lemon and Garlic Dressing

Mix the lemon juice, olive oil and garlic together in a small bowl until smooth. Season to taste with pepper and a little salt.

INGREDIENTS

2 tsp lemon juice

6 tbsp extra virgin olive oil

2 garlic cloves, crushed

salt and freshly ground black pepper

4. Spicy Lime and Honey Dressing

This is delicious with avocados, green leaves and smoked meats.

Mix the lime juice, chilli oil, olive oil and honey in a small bowl until smooth. Season to taste with pepper and a little salt.

INGREDIENTS

2 tbsp lime juice

tbsp chilli-flavoured oil

4 tbsp extra virgin olive oil

2 tsp clear honey

salt and freshly ground black pepper

Avocado and Sesame Seed Salad

This delicious, easy to make salad, creates a perfect side dish.

In a dry frying pan, toast the sesame seeds until golden brown. Empty the salad leaves into a bowl. Snip over the fresh herbs and add the chopped avocado and toasted sesame seeds. Combine all the ingredients for the dressing and season to taste. Pour over the salad and toss to combine.

To prepare: 15 minutes

INGREDIENTS

3 tbsp sesame seeds

1 bag ready-washed salad leaves

fresh herbs (parsley, mint, basil or coriander)

1 ripe avocado, chopped

FOR THE DRESSING

juice of ½ orange

1 tsp lemon juice

1 tbsp olive oil

salt and freshly ground black pepper

Bacon, Blue Cheese and Walnut Salad

SERVES 4-6

This is a deliciously crunchy, textured salad. In place of blue cheese, you could use mature Cheddar or any cheese with a strong flavour.

Heat the oven to 180°C/350°F/gas mark 4 and bake the walnut pieces on a shallow baking tray for 5-6 minutes, stirring often. Do not burn them or they will become bitter. Cut the lettuce into chunks. Rinse the leaves then pat them dry. Trim the bacon rashers, then snip into small pieces with scissors. Fry the bacon gently in a pan with the oil for 1 minute, then drain well on kitchen paper. Crumble the cheese into bite-sized pieces. In a bowl, whisk the vinegar, mustard and seasoning. Add the olive oil and whisk until thickened. Turn the salad leaves into a serving bowl. Add the dressing and toss to cover all the leaves. Sprinkle over the bacon bits, crumbled cheese and walnuts.

To prepare: 10 minutes

To chill: 7 minutes

INGREDIENTS

85g/3oz walnuts, chopped (or snipped with a pair of scissors)

1 lettuce

230g/8oz mixed salad leaves, e.g. oak leaf, lamb's lettuce, watercress

330g/12oz rashers streaky bacon

2 tbsp groundnut oil

230g/8oz blue cheese (e.g. Roquefort, Gorgonzola or Stilton)

FOR THE DRESSING

2 tbsp white wine vinegar

1 tsp grainy mustard

salt and freshly ground black pepper

6 tbsp extra virgin olive oil

Carrot, Olive and Egg Salad

This salad is good with crumbly cheese such as Wensleydale and some dark rye bread.

Make the dressing. In a small bowl, combine 5 tbsp oil, the orange juice and zest and lime or lemon juice, reserving 1-2 tsp. Season to taste. Toss the grated carrot with the dressing until well coated. Leave to stand for 5 minutes. Before serving, snip in the parsley, add the olives, season to taste again and sprinkle with the reserved lemon juice and a little more olive oil. Arrange the quarters of hard-boiled egg over the top and serve.

To prepare: 10 minutes

To chill: 7 minutes

INGREDIENTS

400g/14oz carrots, grated

handful of flat leaf parsley

4 tbsp stoned black olives

4 hard-boiled eggs, quartered

FOR THE DRESSING

5½ tbsp olive oil

1 tbsp juice and pinch of finely grated zest of orange

juice of 1 lime or lemon

sea salt and freshly ground black pepper

SERVES 4

Carrot, Raisin and Almond Salad

A refreshing crunchy salad, with a delicate taste ideal as a side dish.

Make the dressing by whisking the oil, vinegar, honey and mustard together in a bowl. Season with pepper and a little salt. Heat a dry frying pan and toast the almonds until golden brown, stirring constantly. Toss the grated carrot with the almonds, raisins and parsley or coriander, if using, then dress with the honey dressing.

To prepare: 10 minutes

To cook: 7 minutes

INGREDIENTS

55g/2oz almonds

2 large carrots, grated

110g/4oz raisins or currants

2 tbsp chopped parsley or coriander (optional)

FOR THE DRESSING

5 tbsp olive oil

1 tbsp white wine vinegar

1 tbsp honey

1 tsp mustard

salt and freshly ground black pepper

Chicory and Ham Salad with a Mustard Dressing

The sharp taste of the chicory complements the creamy dressing and the smooth taste of the ham.

Prepare the chicory by removing the base of each head and slicing the rest of the chicory finely. Cut the ham slices into thin strips. Put the chicory and ham into a serving dish. Whisk together the vinegar, mustard, crème fraîche and salt and then slowly whisk in the olive oil to make a thick, creamy dressing.

To prepare: 10 minutes

To chill: 5 minutes

INGREDIENTS

4 large heads chicory

8 slices ham
(preferably good-quality honey-roasted)

FOR THE DRESSING

1 tbsp cider or white wine vinegar

1 tbsp Dijon mustard

2 tbsp crème fraîche

pinch of salt

6 tbsp extra virgin olive oil

Greek Salad

In place of Feta cheese, you could use any firm, white, strong-flavoured cheese.

Mix together the cheese, tomatoes, cucumber, onion and olives. Season with the salt and pepper and then drizzle over the olive oil and the lemon juice. Toss well to combine.

To prepare: 10 minutes

INGREDIENTS

170g/6oz Feta cheese, chopped into small pieces

6 ripe, firm tomatoes, cut into eighths

½ cucumber, cut into chunks

1 onion, finely sliced

55g/2oz black olives, stoned

salt and freshly ground black pepper

FOR THE DRESSING

4 tbsp olive oil

juice of 1 lemon

Salade Niçoise

This is a hugely flexible salad which can be varied according to what you have in your kitchen. If you don't have anchovy fillets, capers or cucumber to hand, for example, just leave them out, and if you don't have fresh green beans, use a tin of butter beans, flageolets or kidney beans, drained and rinsed.

Boil the potatoes in a pan of salted water until just tender. Boil the eggs in another pan for 4 minutes if you like them soft, or up to 10 for hard-boiled yolks. Meanwhile, boil or steam the green beans until just tender. Separate the lettuce leaves and rinse well. Pat the leaves dry, then shred them and put in the bottom of a large salad bowl (use 2 if necessary). Trim the spring onions and snip them over the lettuce. Slice the cucumber into chunks and add to the bowl. Halve the tomatoes and add.

Drain the tuna and flake half of it into the salad bowl. Add half the chopped anchovies, capers and olives and sprinkle over half the herbs. Add the green beans. When the eggs and potatoes are cooked, drain the potatoes and leave to cool. Transfer the eggs to a bowl of cold water to stop them from cooking any further. Add the potatoes to the salad. Shell the eggs and cut them into quarters.

To make the dressing, whisk together all the ingredients and season to taste. Pour half the dressing over the salad and toss well to mix. Add the remaining tuna, anchovies, capers and olives and the remaining dressing. Toss again, then decorate with the eggs and the remaining herbs.

INGREDIENTS

450g/1lb salad or new potatoes

6 eggs

110g/4oz green beans, trimmed and halved

1 large crispy lettuce

bunch of spring onions

1 cucumber

450g/1lb cherry tomatoes

400g/14oz tinned tuna chunks in oil

8 anchovy fillets, chopped

2 tbsp capers

230g/8oz stoned black olives

large bunch of chopped fresh parsley (or any other fresh herb e.g. basil, chives, tarragon)

FOR THE DRESSING

2 garlic cloves, crushed

140ml/5fl oz extra virgin olive oil

2 tbsp white wine vinegar

2 tbsp lemon juice

salt and freshly ground black pepper

SERVES 6

Smoked Mackerel and New Potato Salad

SERVES 6

To cook: 10 minutes

To chill: 1 hour

This is an easy recipe which makes an impressive informal supper dish. It's very good with store cupboard ratatouille (see page 77). You could substitute tuna for the smoked mackerel.

Skin the mackerel fillets or drain the tuna, and flake the flesh into chunks. Scrub the potatoes and put them in a pan of boiling salted water. Bring to a simmer, cover and cook until just tender – about 10 minutes. Drain, then shake the potatoes in the pan over the heat to dry them. When cool, cut them into thick slices. Peel and slice the onion, then separate it into rings. Cover the rings with boiling water, then let them stand for 10 minutes. Drain and chill them. In a mixing bowl, combine the soured cream, mustard, wine vinegar and oil. Season with salt and pepper. Add the potatoes, onion and flaked mackerel. Toss until combined well. Leave to marinate for 1 hour or as long as possible. Line a serving bowl with lettuce leaves and turn the potato mixture into it. Sprinkle with chives, if using, and serve.

INGREDIENTS

3 smoked mackerel fillets, or 3 x 185g/6½oz tins of tuna

450g/1lb new potatoes

1 medium onion, or 2 shallots

crisp lettuce, e.g. Iceberg, for serving

2 tsp chopped fresh chives (optional)

FOR THE DRESSING

140ml/5fl oz soured cream

1 level tsp Dijon mustard

1 tbsp white wine vinegar

3 tbsp grapeseed or other mild oil

salt and freshly ground black pepper

Spicy Bean, Chickpea and Pepper Salad

Serve this salad as a light lunch for 4, or as a starter for 6-8 people.

Mix the beans, chickpeas and peppers together in a bowl.

Combine the dressing ingredients, whisking together with a fork. Check the seasoning. Pour the dressing over the bean salad and toss.

To prepare: 10 minutes

INGREDIENTS

1 x 425g/15oz tin red kidney beans, rinsed and drained

1 x 425g/15oz tin chickpeas, rinsed and drained

1 green pepper, seeded and chopped

1 red or yellow pepper, seeded and chopped

FOR THE DRESSING

115ml/4fl oz olive oil

55ml/2fl oz red wine vinegar

3 spring onions, chopped

1 garlic clove, crushed

few drops of Tabasco

1 tsp clear honey

fresh parsley, chopped (optional)

sea salt and freshly ground black pepper, to taste

SERVES 4

Warm Sausage and Potato Salad

To prepare: 10 minutes

To cook: 45 minutes

This is a substantial salad for a cold winter's day, or anytime you feel like comfort food. If you don't have any sausage, substitute salami, crispy bacon bits or other strong-flavoured leftover meat.

Cook the sausages over a very low heat in a pan with a little oil until the flesh is no longer pink and the outsides are brown and crisp. This can take up to 45 minutes. Drain on kitchen paper and cut into thick slices. Meanwhile cook the potatoes in boiling salted water for about 15 minutes until they are done but still firm. Drain and leave to cool. When cool enough to handle, slice into thick chunks. In a small bowl, combine the shallot and garlic with the oil and mayonnaise. Snip in plenty of parsley. Whisk, add the vinegar, whisk again and season well. Tip half the potatoes into a serving bowl. Spoon over half the dressing, add half the sliced sausage and toss lightly until well coated. Add the rest of the potatoes, sausage and dressing and toss again.

INGREDIENTS

4 Italian pork sausages

1 tsp oil

450g/1lb salad potatoes, scrubbed

FOR THE DRESSING

1 shallot, finely chopped

½ garlic clove, crushed

3 tbsp olive oil

1 tbsp good quality mayonnaise

sprigs of flat leaf parsley

2 tsp red or white wine vinegar

sea salt and freshly ground black pepper

Watercress and Satsuma Salad

The sharpness of the watercress and the tangy taste of the satsumas combine effortlessly in this unusual dish which can be served either as a side salad (as here) or with piping hot crusty bread as a more substantial main meal.

Combine the dressing ingredients, then combine the satsumas with the watercress and chives (if using) in a bowl. When ready to serve, toss the salad with the dressing.

To prepare: 10 minutes

INGREDIENTS

12 satsumas, peeled and segments separated

2 x 75g/2½oz packets of ready-prepared watercress

4 tbsp snipped chives (optional)

FOR THE DRESSING

2 tbsp balsamic vinegar

6 tbsp walnut oil

salt and pepper

SERVES
6

MEAT AND POULTRY

Fresh meat is not exactly something you can keep in the cupboard for that last-minute dinner party, but with one ingredient that is freshly bought and some old favourites from the cupboard, you can produce excellent results.

Chicken with a Creamy Garlic Sauce

Heat the oil in a frying pan. Cut the chicken into bite-sized pieces and brown in the hot oil, then remove with a slotted spoon. Fry the onion and garlic gently, until softened but not brown. Add the sliced mushrooms and fry briefly for another 2 minutes. Return the chicken to the pan, add the wine and simmer for 5 minutes, stirring occasionally. Add the cheese and stir gently over low heat until it has melted. Add seasoning to taste. Cook the tagliatelle according to the packet instructions. Serve the chicken spooned over the tagliatelle.

To prepare: 5 minutes

To cook: 15-20 minutes

INGREDIENTS

1 tbsp olive oil

4 skinless chicken breasts

1 large onion, sliced

1 garlic clove, crushed

230g/8oz mushrooms, sliced

½ glass dry white wine

125g/4½ oz garlic and herb cream cheese

salt and freshly ground black pepper

TO SERVE

230g/8oz tagliatelle

Chicken with Bacon, New Potatoes and Mint

Heat ½ tbsp oil in a large frying pan or wok and fry the bacon until crisp. Remove to a strip of kitchen towel. Add the remaining oil and heat, then add the chicken and stir-fry over a high heat until seared all over – about 3-4 minutes. Add the potatoes, turn the heat to medium and continue to stir-fry for 5 minutes or until the potatoes are hot and starting to brown at the edges. Season with salt, pepper and lemon juice, stir in the bacon bits, spring onions and mint and serve at once with peas tossed with butter and fresh mint.

To prepare: 5 minutes

To cook: 10-15 minutes

INGREDIENTS

4½ tbsp extra virgin olive oil

6 rashers bacon, chopped small

6 skinless chicken breasts, cut into strips

1kg/2lb 2oz cooked new potatoes, sliced

salt and pepper

juice of 1 lemon

3 spring onions, finely chopped

3 tbsp chopped mint

TO SERVE

peas with butter and fresh mint

Chilli Con Carne

You could replace the minced beef with a tin of ready cooked mince – in which case omit the flour and stock and simply heat the mince, purée, kidney beans, tomatoes and chilli powder with the fried onion and garlic for a few minutes.

In a large ovenproof casserole, melt the butter and fry the onions and garlic for 10 minutes. Turn the heat up, add the mince and brown it, stirring, for 3 minutes. Add the flour and stir well. Add the tomato purée and stir well, then add the stock, kidney beans, tomatoes and chilli powder and bring to simmering point. Put the lid on the pan, transfer to the oven and cook for about 1¼ hours at 350°F/180°C/Gas Mark 4. Season with salt before serving.

To prepare: 5 minutes

To cook: 1½ hours

INGREDIENTS

55g/2oz butter

2 onions, finely diced

1 garlic clove, crushed

450g/1lb minced beef

1 tbsp flour

2 tbsp tomato purée

570ml/1 pint beef or chicken stock

1 x 425g/15oz tin kidney beans, drained

1 x 425g/15oz tin chopped tomatoes

2 tsp chilli powder

salt and freshly ground black pepper

TO SERVE

cornbread or rice, grated cheese and sour cream

SERVES 4

Quick Stroganoff

You can adapt this recipe for beef, pork fillet or bacon.

Cut the beef, pork or bacon into strips. Heat the oil and the butter in a wok or frying pan, add the meat, spring onions and mushrooms and stir-fry for 6 minutes. Add the sherry, the tomato purée, lemon juice and sour cream and a good grinding of pepper. Simmer for 1-2 minutes, check the seasoning and serve.

To prepare: 5 minutes

To cook: 10 minutes

TO SERVE

noodles, rice or pasta

INGREDIENTS

450g/1lb beef steak, pork fillet or thick slices of good quality bacon, de-rinded

1 tbsp olive oil

30g/1oz butter

2 spring onions, chopped

55g/2oz mushrooms, sliced

2 tbsp sherry or sweet white wine

1 tsp tomato purée

2 tsp lemon juice

140ml/5fl oz sour cream

salt and freshly ground black pepper

Sausages with Onion Gravy

Cook the sausages by grilling or frying them to your liking. While they are cooking, heat the oil in a frying pan, add the onions and sprinkle the sugar over the top. Cook for 10-15 minutes over a medium heat, stirring constantly so the sugar does not stick and burn. When the onions have turned golden brown, sprinkle in the flour and stir to combine. Add the stock gradually, then the red wine and stir to a smooth sauce. Simmer for 2 minutes, add the mustard to your liking and stir well. Season to taste and serve with the sausages and mashed potatoes.

To prepare: 5 minutes

To cook: 30 minutes

INGREDIENTS

450g/1lb pork sausages

2 tbsp olive oil

4 onions, thinly sliced

1 tsp sugar

½ tbsp flour

425ml/15fl oz chicken or beef stock

115ml/4fl oz red wine

salt and freshly ground black pepper

1-2 tbsp grainy mustard

TO SERVE

mashed potatoes

QUICK FISH SAUCE

INGREDIENTS

½ cup bottled mayonnaise

4 tbsp ketchup

2 tbsp lemon juice

2 tbsp sweet pickle

Mix the ingredients together and serve cold with fish fingers, fried fish or fish cakes.

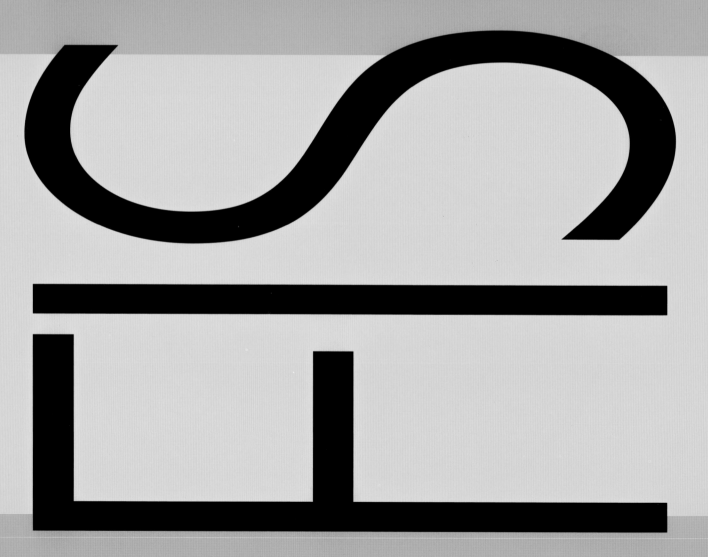

Baked Cod with Lemon

Preheat the oven to 425°F/220°C/gas mark 7. Place each cod steak on a piece of foil large enough to wrap it up. Squeeze lemon juice over the top, dot with butter and season with salt and pepper. Close up the foil so you have four sealed parcels. Bake for 20-25 minutes.

To prepare: 5 minutes

To cook: 20-25 minutes

INGREDIENTS

4 fresh cod steaks (or frozen steaks, thawed) each about 200g/7oz

juice of 1 lemon

55g/2oz butter

salt and freshly ground black pepper

TO SERVE

new potatoes and a green salad

SERVES 4

Grilled Trout with Almonds

Dry the trout with kitchen paper and dust with the seasoned flour. Lay the trout on a grill pan lined with foil and pour a little melted butter over the top. Grill for 10-15 minutes, turning the fish half-way through. Melt the rest of the butter in a small pan and fry the almonds in it until pale golden. Add the lemon juice and season with salt and pepper. Serve the trout with the almond butter poured over the top and with lemon wedges.

To prepare: 5 minutes

To cook: 10-15 minutes

INGREDIENTS

4 fresh or frozen trout, thawed if frozen

1 tbsp flour, seasoned with salt and pepper

55g/2oz melted butter

55g/2oz butter

55g/2oz flaked almonds

juice of ½ lemon

salt and freshly milled black pepper

TO SERVE

lemon wedges

almond butter

Salmon Fish Cakes

If you don't have any salmon, tuna can be substituted.

Cook the potatoes in boiling salted water for 15-20 minutes until tender. Drain and turn into a large bowl, add the butter and the cream and mash until smooth. Add the flaked salmon, parsley, dill, lemon juice, salt and pepper to taste and stir to combine. Lightly flour a working surface, then form the fish mixture into flat cakes with your hands (the mixture should make about 8 cakes, 7cm/3in in diameter). Dip each cake into the beaten egg, then coat with the breadcrumbs. Heat a little oil in a frying pan and fry the fish cakes 2 or 3 at a time until golden brown. Serve with fish sauce (see recipe on page 46) or tartare sauce and a green salad.

To prepare: 10 minutes

To cook: 20-30 minutes

INGREDIENTS

450g/1lb potatoes

55g/2oz butter

3 tbsp double cream

2 x 185g/6½oz tins red salmon

2 tbsp chopped fresh parsley

½ tsp dried dill

1 tbsp lemon juice

salt and freshly ground black pepper

1 egg, beaten

170g/6oz fresh breadcrumbs

plain flour

2 tbsp sunflower oil

TO SERVE

fish sauce, tomato sauce or tartare sauce and a green salad

Rice keeps for ages (although do beware of weevils in the long term!), and, along with pasta, is the store cupboard cook's best friend.

Basmati Rice with Pine Nuts and Sultanas

Serve this with a tomato salad or green leaf and herb salad and chutney for a light main course.

Rinse the rice in a sieve under cold running water. Melt the butter with the oil in a large pan over a moderate heat. Add the rice and raisins and stir to combine. Bring the stock to boil in a saucepan, then add to the rice with a pinch of salt and bring back to the boil. Cover and simmer gently for 8-10 minutes or until all the stock has been absorbed and the rice is tender. Meanwhile, toast the pine nuts in a dry frying pan, stirring continuously, until golden brown. Snip over the fresh herbs, stir in the pine nuts and season to taste.

To prepare: 5 minutes

To cook: 15-20 minutes

INGREDIENTS

230g/8oz basmati rice

55g/2oz butter

2 tbsp oil

55g/2oz raisins

55g/2oz pine nuts

455ml/16fl oz chicken or vegetable stock

salt

2 or 3 sprigs fresh coriander

salt and pepper

Brown Rice with
Soy Sauce and Green Vegetables

Cook the brown rice according to the packet instructions. Meanwhile, cook the peas and the broccoli until tender. When the rice is ready, mix in the peas and broccoli and stir in the spring onions. Add a dash of soy sauce to taste and serve immediately.

To prepare: 5 minutes

To cook: 20-25 minutes

INGREDIENTS

110g/4oz brown rice

110g/4oz frozen peas

110g/4oz broccoli, cut into florets

3 spring onions, chopped

soy sauce, to taste

Chicken and Almond Rice

Cook the rice according to the packet instructions. Blanch the mangetouts in boiling water for 2-3 minutes, then drain. Toast the almonds in a dry frying pan, stirring constantly, until golden brown. Heat the oil in a frying pan, add the onion and red pepper and fry gently to soften – about 10 minutes. Stir in the garlic and fry for another 2-3 minutes. Add the onion, red pepper and garlic to the cooked rice, then gently stir in the chicken, spring onions, the mangetouts and the chopped mint, if using. Season to taste with salt and pepper and a little lemon juice. Turn into a serving dish and sprinkle with the toasted almonds.

To prepare: 10 minutes

To cook: 25-30 minutes

INGREDIENTS

230g/8oz long-grain brown rice

230g/8oz mangetouts, trimmed

55g/2oz flaked almonds

2 tbsp olive oil

1 medium onion, chopped

1 red pepper, de-seeded and chopped

1 garlic clove, chopped

3 cooked chicken breasts, cut into chunks

6-8 spring onions, chopped

small bunch of mint or other fresh herb, finely chopped (optional)

salt and freshly ground black pepper

½ tbsp lemon juice, or to taste

Chicken Liver Risotto

Chicken livers are reasonably cheap and can easily be frozen.

In a heavy-bottomed pan or frying pan, heat half the butter and fry the onion over a low heat until it is soft but not brown. Add the chicken livers and cook gently for 2-3 minutes. Add the rice and stir until each grain is coated with fat. Add the wine and cook for 1 minute until it has either evaporated or been absorbed by the rice. Add 1 ladleful of stock and the tomato purée and cook, until the liquid has been absorbed. Keep adding stock, a ladleful at a time, letting the rice absorb the liquid each time and stirring continuously. Do not flood the rice. After about 20 minutes, the risotto should be creamy and the grains of rice still firm to the bite. Once the rice is cooked, remove the pan from the heat and stir in the Parmesan cheese. Cover the pan and leave to rest for 2 minutes before serving. Scatter with the chopped parsley or more Parmesan.

INGREDIENTS

55g/2oz unsalted butter

½ onion, finely chopped

230g/8oz chicken livers, chopped

230g/8oz risotto rice (arborio)

¼ glass red wine

855ml/1½ pint chicken stock

1 tsp tomato purée

30g/1oz freshly grated Parmesan cheese

TO SERVE

a few sprigs of fresh parsley, leaves finely chopped or freshly grated Parmesan (optional)

To prepare: 10 minutes

To cook: 25-30 minutes

Mediterranean Wild Rice

The ingredients in this recipe are a moveable feast – vary them according to your taste or what you have available.

Cook the rice according to the packet instructions, rinse in cold running water and set aside. Toast the pine nuts by heating a dry frying pan, adding the nuts and tossing constantly until golden brown. Add the pine nuts, cucumber, pepper, tomatoes, sultanas and mint to the rice and mix to combine. Combine the olive oil and vinegar and season to taste. Toss the rice salad with the dressing and sprinkle the Parmesan over the top to serve.

To prepare: 5 minutes

To cook: 20-25 minutes

INGREDIENTS

230g/8oz wild rice

2 tbsp pine nuts

½ cucumber, chopped

1 yellow pepper, deseeded and diced

8 cherry tomatoes, quartered

55g/2oz sultanas

small bunch of mint, chopped

FOR THE SAUCE

3 tbsp olive oil

1 tbsp white wine vinegar

salt and freshly ground black pepper

55g/2oz Parmesan, grated

Parmesan and Butter Risotto

To prepare: 5 minutes

To cook: 25-30 minutes

Keep the stock simmering in a separate pan so that when it is added it does not slow down the cooking process.

In a heavy-bottomed pan or frying pan, fry the onion in half the butter for about 10 minutes over a low heat until it is soft but not brown. Add the rice and stir until each grain is coated with fat. Add a ladleful of stock and stir. Continue to stir until the rice has absorbed all the liquid. Keep adding stock, a ladleful at a time, letting the rice absorb the liquid each time and stirring continuously. It should take about 20 minutes, by which time the risotto should be creamy and the grains of rice still firm to the bite. At this stage, stir in the remaining butter and the cheese. Taste and adjust the seasoning, then cover and leave to rest for about 3 minutes before serving. Scatter with the chopped parsley, and extra Parmesan, if liked.

INGREDIENTS

1 onion, finely chopped

85g/3oz unsalted butter

450g/1lb 2oz risotto rice (arborio)

1.4 litre/2½ pt chicken stock

55g/2oz Parmesan cheese

salt and freshly ground black pepper

TO SERVE

a few sprigs of fresh parsley, leaves finely chopped and freshly grated Parmesan (optional)

Pea Risotto

To prepare: 5 minutes

To cook: 25-30 minutes

Put the peas in a pan of simmering water, leave for 30 seconds and drain. Rinse with cold water to stop the cooking process. In a heavy-bottomed pan, fry the onion in half the butter over a very low heat until it is soft but not brown. Add the rice and stir until each grain is coated with fat. Add the wine and cook for 1 minute until it has either evaporated or been absorbed by the rice. Add 1 ladleful of stock and cook, stirring constantly, until all the liquid has been absorbed. Keep adding stock, a ladleful at a time, letting the rice absorb the liquid each time and stirring continuously. Do not flood the rice.

After about 10 minutes, add the peas, then continue adding stock in the same way. After another 8-10 minutes, the risotto should be ready. It should be creamy, with the grains of rice still firm to the bite. Once the rice is cooked, remove the pan from the heat and stir in the Parmesan cheese and the remaining butter. Cover the pan and leave to rest for 2 minutes before serving.

INGREDIENTS

140g/5oz frozen peas

55g/2oz unsalted butter

½ onion, finely chopped

230g/8oz risotto rice (arborio)

¼ glass white wine

855ml/1½ pint chicken stock

30g/1oz freshly grated Parmesan cheese

TO SERVE

sprigs of fresh parsley, finely chopped leaves or freshly grated Parmesan (optional)

SERVES 2

PASTA

The blank canvas of pasta, like the crunchy green leaves of a salad, is a perfect foil for rich, strong flavours. To a pan of steaming, slippery, just-cooked pasta, you are free to add almost anything you like – it is the perfect store cupboard food. As a guideline, if pasta is the main element of a dish, you will need about 110g/4oz per person; for 4 use 450g/1lb.

FIVE SPEEDY IDEAS

- Add butter, olive oil, crushed garlic browned in butter, chopped herbs and a squeeze of lemon juice to a bowl of hot pasta
- Toss in toasted pine nuts or flaked almonds with some goat's cheese or freshly grated Parmesan
- Add strips of honey-roast ham with some chopped parsley, crushed garlic fried in butter and, 1 tbsp of crème fraîche
- Toss hot pasta with cooked spinach (from a tin) mixed with 1 tbsp green pesto, a grinding of fresh nutmeg, 1 tbsp crème fraîche and a squeeze of lemon juice
- Mix cooked peas with hot pasta and a dressing of butter, balsamic vinegar and pepper. Snip in some spring onions or chives

Cherry Tomato, Basil and Feta Cheese Pasta

If you don't have Feta use another strong-flavoured cheese or leave it out altogether. Make sure the tomatoes are at room temperature before adding them to the pasta.

Cook the pasta according to the packet instructions. When it is ready, drain it, add the oil and toss to coat. Add the tomatoes, Feta cheese and basil, toss again, then add the balsamic vinegar and some seasoning, to taste. Serve immediately with the grated Parmesan.

To prepare: 5 minutes

To cook: 10-15 minutes

SERVES 2

INGREDIENTS

230g/8oz penne or other pasta

1 tbsp olive oil

8 cherry tomatoes, quartered

200g/7oz Feta cheese, crumbled

small bunch basil, torn

3 tsp balsamic vinegar, to taste

salt and freshly ground black pepper

TO SERVE

freshly grated Parmesan (optional)

Chicken and Mushroom Tagliatelle

In a medium saucepan, heat 1 tbsp oil with the butter and gently sauté the onion. Add the mushrooms and cook until soft. Remove the mushrooms from the pan with their juices and keep warm. If necessary, add a little more oil to the pan, then add the chicken strips and stir-fry briefly until white but not cooked through. Add the sherry, vermouth or wine, if using, and cook until it is absorbed. Stir in the flour and cook for 1 minute more. Pour in the stock, bring to the boil, stirring until thickened and smooth. Simmer for 10 minutes and season well. Meanwhile, cook the pasta according to the packet instructions, drain it and toss with 1 tbsp olive oil. Toast the almonds: heat a dry frying pan, add the almonds and stir constantly until golden brown. Do not allow them to burn. Remove from the pan when ready. Mix the cream or crème fraîche and almonds into the chicken and sauce and gently reheat. Stir in the cooked pasta and serve hot, sprinkled with some Parmesan cheese and parsley.

To prepare: 5 minutes

To cook: 15-20 minutes

INGREDIENTS

230g/8oz tagliatelle

2 tbsp olive oil

30g/1oz butter

1 onion, sliced

230g/8oz mushrooms, sliced

4 chicken breasts, cut into thin strips

3 tbsp dry sherry, vermouth or white wine (optional)

2 tbsp flour

570ml/1 pint chicken stock

3 tbsp flaked almonds

140ml/5fl oz double cream or crème fraîche

salt and freshly ground black pepper

TO SERVE

freshly grated Parmesan and chopped fresh parsley

Flo's Moroccan Sauce

This sauce is good with pasta, and excellent with couscous – use the instant type that just needs soaking in stock.

In a frying pan, fry the onion and garlic gently in the oil until soft but not brown. Add the sardines and their tomato sauce to the pan, mash them down with a fork and fry gently for 2 minutes. Add the chopped tomatoes and tomato purée and stir to mix, then cook for 3 minutes. Meanwhile, peel the orange and remove as much pith as possible. Cut the flesh into small chunks and add these and the orange juice to the pan together with the raisins. Cook gently for another 10-15 minutes. While the sauce is cooking, prepare the pasta or couscous according to the packet instructions. Heat a dry frying pan and toast the pine nuts, stirring constantly, until they are golden brown. Season the sauce to taste and serve scattered with the chopped mint and toasted pine nuts.

To prepare: 5 minutes

To cook: 20-25 minutes

INGREDIENTS

1 medium onion, finely diced

1 garlic clove, finely chopped

1 tsp olive oil

1 small tin sardines in tomato sauce

1 x 400g/14oz tin chopped tomatoes

1 tsp tomato purée

1 large orange

85g/3oz raisins

230g/8oz pasta or 110g/4oz instant couscous

TO SERVE

55g/2oz toasted pine nuts, fresh mint, finely chopped

SERVES
2

Gnocchi with Broccoli and Mushrooms

Gnocchi are not pasta – they are Italian potato dumplings, which are sold vacuum packed in most large supermarkets. However, they serve the same function as pasta, being deliciously bland and filling, and complement a garlicky sauce such as this. If you don't have or can't find them, substitute with penne or other short, stubby pasta.

Steam or boil the broccoli florets for about 5 minutes until tender but with a slight crunch. Wipe the mushrooms and chop finely. Heat the butter in a pan, add the mushrooms and the garlic and cook for 4-5 minutes until they are soft and have given off plenty of juices. Cook the gnocchi in a large pan of boiling water. They are ready when they float to the surface. Drain, and return to the pan. Add the broccoli and the mushrooms together with all the garlic and juices from the pan. Squeeze over the lemon juice, stir in the Parmesan and season.

INGREDIENTS

110g/4oz broccoli florets

110g/4oz mushrooms

30g/1oz butter

1 garlic clove, chopped

1 x 400g/14oz pack of gnocchi

squeeze of lemon juice

55g/2oz Parmesan, freshly grated

salt and freshly ground black pepper

To prepare: 5 minutes

To cook: 15-20 minutes

Mushroom Tagliatelle

Wipe the mushrooms and slice them thinly. Melt the butter in a large pan, add the garlic and mushrooms. Cover the pan and gently cook the mushrooms for about 15 minutes. Add the wine and seasoning, stir and continue to cook, uncovered, for about 5-7 minutes or until the liquid has reduced and darkened. While the mushrooms are cooking, prepare the pasta or noodles according to the packet instructions. Stir the parsley into the sauce, place the pasta on plates and serve the mushrooms on top. You can decorate with parsley or sprinkle over some freshly ground Parmesan cheese.

To prepare: 5 minutes

To cook: 20-25 minutes

INGREDIENTS

1kg/2lb 2oz large flat mushrooms

170g/6oz butter

2 garlic cloves, crushed

2 glasses red wine

salt and freshly ground black pepper

450g/1lb tagliatelle or dried egg noodles

small bunch of parsley, chopped

TO SERVE

freshly grated Parmesan or parsley (optional)

SERVES 4

Quick Spaghetti and Tomato Sauce

Warm the oil in a frying pan. Add the onion and chopped garlic and cook gently without letting it colour. Add the tomatoes and the thyme or oregano, bring briefly to the boil, reduce the heat and let it stew gently, uncovered, until the sauce has reduced and thickened. Season to taste. Cook the spaghetti according to the packet instructions, then drain and toss with a little oil.

Tip the spaghetti into a bowl and toss with the tomato sauce. Serve with the grated Parmesan.

To prepare: 5 minutes

To cook: 10-15 minutes

INGREDIENTS

2 tbsp olive oil, plus extra for tossing with spaghetti

1 small onion, chopped

1 garlic clove, finely chopped

1 x 400g/14oz tin tomatoes

½ tsp dried thyme or oregano

salt and freshly ground black pepper

450g/1lb spaghetti

freshly grated Parmesan

Spaghetti alla Carbonara

Cook the spaghetti according to the packet instructions. Meanwhile, heat the olive oil in a small saucepan, add the bacon and fry till the fat starts to run. Whisk the eggs in a bowl with the cream, if using, add a good grinding of black pepper and 2 tbsp of the Parmesan cheese. When the pasta is cooked, drain it and return it to the hot saucepan off the heat. Stir in the beaten eggs, the bacon and the oil from the pan until all the pasta is coated with egg (it will start to set slightly). Serve with the extra Parmesan cheese sprinkled over the top.

To prepare: 5 minutes

To cook: 10-15 minutes

INGREDIENTS

230g/8oz spaghetti

1 tbsp olive oil

110g/4oz streaky bacon, de-rinded and chopped

2 large eggs

2 tbsp double cream (optional)

salt and freshly ground black pepper

3 tbsp freshly grated Parmesan

SERVES 2

Spaghetti with Olives and Anchovies

To make the sauce, heat the oil in a medium saucepan, add the garlic and basil. Cook briefly until the garlic has just started to turn golden. Add all the other sauce ingredients, stir and season with some pepper. Turn down the heat and let the sauce simmer gently, uncovered, for about 40 minutes, until it has reduced and thickened to a rich sauce.

About 10 minutes before the sauce is ready, cook the spaghetti according to the packet instructions, drain and return to the saucepan. If the sauce is not quite ready, stir in a little olive oil with the pasta to prevent it from sticking together. Mix the sauce with the spaghetti and more chopped fresh basil, and Parmesan cheese.

To prepare: 5 minutes

To cook: 45 minutes

INGREDIENTS

230g/8oz spaghetti

½ tbsp olive oil, plus extra for tossing with spaghetti

2 garlic cloves, finely chopped

1 tsp fresh basil, or 1 tsp dried basil

55g/2oz anchovies, drained

110g/4oz pitted black olives, roughly chopped

110g/4oz pitted green olives, roughly chopped

1 tsp chilli powder

1 x 400g/14oz tin chopped tomatoes

1 tbsp tomato purée

1 tsp red wine vinegar

2 tbsp extra virgin olive oil

salt and freshly ground black pepper

TO SERVE

chopped fresh basil, freshly grated Parmesan cheese (optional)

SERVES 2

Spinach and Blue Cheese Sauce with Pasta

If you don't have fresh spinach, use half a 400g/14oz tin of cooked spinach. Drain it of any liquid, add to a pan with the blue cheese and cream and cook as below.

Cook the pasta according to the packet instructions. Wash the spinach thoroughly, then tear the leaves up and place in a pan over medium heat with the water still clinging to the leaves. Cover the pan and cook until the spinach has wilted – about 2 minutes. Add the blue cheese and the cream and cook gently until the cheese has melted. Season to taste and add a squeeze of lemon juice to sharpen. Serve immediately with the pasta.

To prepare: 5 minutes

To cook: 10-15 minutes

INGREDIENTS

230g/8oz pasta

140g/5oz baby spinach leaves, washed and shredded

170g/6oz soft blue cheese, cubed

285ml/10fl oz single cream

squeeze of lemon juice

salt and freshly ground black pepper

SERVES 2

STIR-FRIES

With very little effort, a bit of imagination and just about anything you can find in the cupboard, you can produce an interesting and impressive stir-fry.

Chicken Strips with Sesame Seeds

You can serve this deliciously tangy dish with noodles, rice or pasta – or on top of a green salad of mixed leaves.

Heat the oil in a wok and stir-fry the sesame seeds with the spring onions for 1 minute. Add the chicken and stir-fry for another 5 minutes. Stir in the soy sauce and the chilli sauce, then add the coriander, if using, and the sesame oil. Season to taste and serve on a bed of rice or noodles.

To prepare: 5 minutes

To cook: 5 minutes

INGREDIENTS

1 tbsp sunflower oil

1-2 tbsp sesame seeds

2 spring onions, chopped

2 skinned chicken breasts, cut into strips or chunks

1 tbsp soy sauce

few drops of chilli sauce or one or two fresh chillies, chopped

coriander leaves, roughly chopped (optional)

1 tsp sesame oil

TO SERVE

rice, noodles, or pasta

Chinese Chicken Stir-fry

Place the chicken strips in a dish. Mix the cornflour with the soy sauce in a cup, then pour it over the chicken and leave to marinate for 30 minutes to 1 hour if possible (the longer the better). Heat the oil in a wok, add the chicken and cook briefly on all sides. Transfer to a plate. Add the onion, garlic, ginger, broccoli, mushrooms and spring onions and stir-fry for 2 minutes. Add a little salt to taste, then return the chicken to the pan, add the sherry, cover with a lid and cook for a further 3-4 minutes. Meanwhile, cook the noodles according to the packet instructions. Drain and toss with the soy sauce to taste. Serve the chicken on a bed of noodles.

To prepare: 30 minutes

To cook: 10 minutes

INGREDIENTS

2 skinned chicken breasts, cut into strips

1 tbsp cornflour

140ml/5fl oz soy sauce, plus 1 tbsp for tossing with noodles

1 tbsp sunflower oil

½ onion, finely chopped

1 garlic clove, finely chopped

½ tbsp grated fresh ginger

85g/3oz broccoli, sliced

85g/3oz mushrooms, sliced

2 spring onions, finely chopped

salt

1 tbsp sherry

TO SERVE

egg noodles

Fast Sweet and Sour Stir-fry

Heat the oil in a wok and stir-fry the peppers and onions for about 4 minutes. In a separate bowl, mix together the pineapple juice, tomato purée, soy sauce, vinegar and cornflour. Add to the vegetables and bring to the boil. Simmer for 2 minutes. Add the remaining ingredients and stir-fry for another 2 minutes. Serve with rice or noodles.

To prepare: 5 minutes

To cook: 5-10 minutes

INGREDIENTS

2 tbsp sunflower oil

1 red or yellow pepper, deseeded and diced

1 green pepper, deseeded and diced

small bunch spring onions, chopped

200g/7oz tin pineapple chunks, plus 3 tbsp juice

1 tbsp tomato purée

2 tbsp soy sauce

1 tbsp white wine vinegar

2 tsp cornflour

handful of cashew nuts, peanuts or pine nuts

200g/7oz bean sprouts

TO SERVE

rice or noodles

To prepare: 5 minutes

To cook: 15-20 minutes

Prawn and Egg Stir-fried Rice

Make sure you defrost the prawns thoroughly before you start cooking.

Beat the eggs gently in a cup or small bowl with a seasoning of salt and pepper. Heat a small frying pan, add the butter and when it foams, pour in the egg mixture. Cook over a medium heat, tilting the pan from time to time so that any runny egg mixture is evenly distributed. Continue cooking until the egg is set, then carefully flip the omelette to cook the underside. Don't worry if it breaks up – you will be slicing it up anyway. Slide the omelette on to a chopping board and slice into thin strips. Cook the rice according to the packet instructions, drain and set aside. Heat the oil in a wok, then stir in the garlic and the spring onions and stir-fry for 2 minutes. Add the prawns and stir for 1-2 minutes to heat through. Add the cooked rice and stir again, then the strips of omelette.

INGREDIENTS

2 eggs

salt and freshly ground black pepper

knob of butter

110g/4oz white rice

1 tbsp sunflower oil

1 garlic clove, finely chopped

3 spring onions, finely chopped

170g/6oz cooked peeled prawns,
defrosted if frozen

TO SERVE

soy sauce (optional)

Vegetable Stir-fry

Vary the ingredients in this dish according to the vegetables you have available – use this recipe as a guide.

Cook the noodles according to the packet instructions. Drain, toss with the soy sauce to taste, then set aside. Heat the oil in a wok, add the mangetouts, carrots, pepper, sweet corn, garlic and ginger and stir-fry for 2 minutes. Add the bean sprouts, chilli sauce and stock and stir-fry for another 2-3 minutes. Serve with the noodles. Sprinkle with a little sesame oil and snip some fresh herbs or spring onions over the top.

To prepare: 5 minutes

To cook: 5 minutes

INGREDIENTS

170g/6oz dried egg noodles

1 tbsp soy sauce

1 tbsp sunflower oil

110g/4oz mangetouts, trimmed

55g/2oz carrots, sliced diagonally

half a red pepper, sliced

55g/2oz baby sweetcorn, left whole

1 garlic clove, crushed

½ tbsp grated fresh ginger

55g/2oz bean sprouts

few drops of chilli sauce

2 tbsp vegetable stock or water

TO SERVE

sesame oil and fresh herbs or spring onions (optional)

Although, most vegetables don't keep well, they can be jazzed up quickly with any number of store cupboard ingredients.

Alice's Potatoes

This dish is best prepared the night before so that the flavours have a chance to mingle. If you're short of time, leave it to stand for 1 hour or as long as possible. Serve with a green salad and a garlicky dressing.

Peel the potatoes and cut them in half. Cook in boiling salted water for approx 20 minutes or until just tender. Drain and cool slightly. Grate the potatoes coarsely into a large bowl. Add the sour cream, chopped shallots, half the grated cheese, the salt and the pepper. Place in a greased casserole dish. Top with the remaining cheese and sprinkle with the paprika. Cover and refrigerate overnight, if possible, or for at least 1 hour if short of time. Preheat the oven to 180°C/350°F/gas mark 4. Bake, uncovered, for 35 minutes or until the top is golden and crisp.

To prepare: 1 hour

To cook: 35-40 minutes

INGREDIENTS

6 large potatoes

285ml/10fl oz sour cream

8 shallots, finely chopped

170g/6oz grated Cheddar cheese

salt and freshly ground black pepper

1 tsp paprika

Baked Potatoes

Baked potatoes are endlessly versatile
vegetables. There are almost as many fillings
as there are recipes in the world when it
comes to baked potatoes. Often the best way
of serving them is with some good unsalted
butter and a generous seasoning of sea salt
and freshly ground black pepper.

Toppings

If you like, you can scoop the flesh out of the cooked
potato and mix it with one of the following suggestions
before serving in its jacket.

BASIC METHOD

Maris Piper baking potatoes: Scrub the potatoes
and dry them thoroughly. Prick 2 or 3 times with
a fork. Brush with a little olive oil and sprinkle with
salt. If time is short, push a metal skewer through
the potatoes. Bake for 1¼ hours at
180°C/350°F/gas mark 4 or until the skins are
crispy and the flesh soft.

SWEET POTATOES

Bake as above, but put the potatoes on a tray to
catch the juices that emerge during cooking.

Pesto sauce and butter

Prawn cocktail mix: cooked prawns combined
with mayonnaise, tomato purée,
Worcestershire sauce and black pepper

Sour cream and snipped chives

Ham, butter and black pepper

Mushrooms cooked in butter and garlic

Parsley, garlic and olive oil

Baked beans and grated Cheddar cheese

Ratatouille

This dish will keep very well for a few days in the fridge – in fact, the flavours improve over time. Serve it with baked potatoes or brown rice.

Heat the oil in a heavy-based pan and fry the onions until soft but not brown. Add the aubergines, stir and cook for 1-2 minutes, then add the courgettes and stir and cook them for another 1-2 minutes. Add the peppers, stir again for 1-2 minutes, then finish with the garlic. Add more oil if necessary and cook for 2 more minutes. Cover the pan and cook gently for 40 minutes. Add the tomatoes, the tomato purée and the seasoning and cook for another 30 minutes until the vegetables are soft but not mushy. Just before serving, stir in the herbs and, 1-2 tbsp red wine.

To prepare: 5 minutes

To cook: 1½ hours

INGREDIENTS

6 tbsp olive oil, plus more if necessary

2 medium onions, sliced

2 small aubergines, diced

2 courgettes, sliced

2 red peppers, diced

3 garlic cloves, crushed

2 × 400g/14oz tins chopped tomatoes

2 tbsp tomato purée

salt and freshly ground black pepper

chopped fresh or dried herbs

1-2 tbsp red wine (optional)

SERVES 4

Roasted Vegetables

Roasting vegetables renders them deliciously sweet and tender. You can vary the mixture of vegetables to suit what you have available. Serve with couscous or rice for a main course or, if you prefer, roast some small salad potatoes with the other vegetables.

Preheat the oven to 190°C/375°F/gas mark 5. Chop the carrots and the parsnips in half if large. Arrange all the vegetables on a roasting dish in one layer, pour over enough olive oil to coat them all and season with salt and pepper. Roast the vegetables for 50-60 minutes, stirring half-way through. Serve with rice or couscous and 1 tbsp pesto sauce per person.

To prepare: 5 minutes

To cook: 1 hour

INGREDIENTS

230g/8oz carrots, peeled

230g/8oz parsnips, peeled

230g/8oz courgettes, roughly sliced

2 red peppers, de-seeded and quartered

2 green peppers, de-seeded and quartered

8 garlic cloves, unpeeled

330g/12oz shallots, unpeeled

extra virgin olive oil

salt and freshly ground black pepper

TO SERVE

4 tbsp pesto sauce

Stuffed Peppers

Serve these peppers with a green salad and some good bread for a light lunch.

Preheat the oven to 220°C/425°F/gas mark 7. Halve the peppers and scoop out the seeds and pith. Cut the tomatoes into quarters and put these into the peppers. Chop up the anchovies and sprinkle over the tomatoes. Add 1 tbsp good olive oil and a little crushed garlic to each pepper. Bake for about 25-30 minutes until the peppers are wilted and brown in places. Serve garnished with the parsley.

To prepare: 5 minutes

To cook: 25-30 minutes

INGREDIENTS

4 red peppers

4 cherry tomatoes

16 anchovy fillets

4 tbsp olive oil

2 garlic cloves, crushed

TO SERVE

finely chopped parsley

SERVES 4

Apart from saving on the washing up, one pot meals are a great way of using up any number of store cupboard ingredients.

Cheesy Bean and Sausage Bake

This is a hearty winter dish that children – and most adults – will love.

Preheat the oven to 200°C/400°F/gas mark 6. Fry the onion and garlic in the oil until soft but not brown. Stir in the beans, tomatoes, tomato purée and sausages. Turn the mixture into an ovenproof dish, top with the grated cheese and herbs and cook for 30 minutes.

To prepare: 5 minutes

To cook: 30 minutes

INGREDIENTS

1 onion, finely chopped

garlic clove, crushed

1 tbsp olive oil

1 × 400g/14oz tin butter beans, drained

1 × 400g/14oz tin chopped tomatoes

1 tbsp tomato purée

4 cooked sausages, sliced

55g/2oz Cheddar cheese, grated

fresh herbs, finely chopped

Crispy Chicken Bake

Preheat the oven to 350°F/180°C/gas mark 4. Heat the oil in a frying pan and gently fry the onion and pepper for a few minutes until soft but not brown. Toss in a bowl with the chicken, celery, chicken soup, mayonnaise and lemon juice. Turn the mixture into a buttered ovenproof dish. Open the crisp bag but do not remove the crisps. Fold over the open end of the bag, then roll over the crisps with a rolling pin to crush them. In a bowl, mix together the cheese and the crisps and sprinkle over the top of the dish. Bake for 25 minutes or until the top is golden brown and bubbling.

To prepare: 5 minutes

To cook: 30-35 minutes

INGREDIENTS

1 tbsp olive oil

1 large onion, finely diced

1 green pepper, diced

4 cooked chicken breasts, chopped

4 sticks celery, chopped

1 x 300g/10½oz tin concentrated chicken soup

8 tbsp mayonnaise

4 tbsp lemon juice

110g/4oz grated Cheddar cheese

1 small bag ready salted crisps

Macaroni Cheese

The ultimate in comfort food and very easy to make.

Butter a gratin dish, then cook the macaroni according to the packet instructions. Melt the butter in a saucepan over a medium heat, then stir in the flour and mustard powder and cook, still stirring, for about 3 minutes. Remove the pan from the heat and pour in the milk gradually, stirring constantly. Return the pan to the heat, cook the sauce for 5 minutes, stirring constantly, then remove from the heat and stir in 150g/5oz of the cheese. When the macaroni has cooked, drain it thoroughly and add it to the cheese sauce. Season to taste, then pour into the serving dish and sprinkle with the remaining cheese and the breadcrumbs. Put the dish under a hot grill to brown the top, then serve.

To prepare: 5 minutes

To cook: 15-20 minutes

INGREDIENTS

230g/8oz macaroni

55g/2oz butter, plus extra for greasing

3 tbsp flour

1 tsp mustard powder

570ml/1 pint milk

230g/8oz Cheddar cheese, grated

2-3 tbsp breadcrumbs

To prepare: 5 minutes

To cook: 1 hour

Potato and Anchovy Gratin

Preheat the oven to 220°C/425°F/gas mark 7. Peel the onion, halve and slice it finely. Peel the potatoes and slice them finely. Grease a gratin dish with butter – it should be large enough to hold the potatoes to a depth of about 5cm/2in. Lay half the potatoes on the base and scatter over half of the onion, then lay half of the anchovy fillets on top. Arrange the remaining potatoes over the anchovies. Press down with your hand, then add the rest of the onion and anchovies. Mix the vegetable stock with the cream, season with pepper and pour this over the potatoes. The liquid should cover them by about half. Spoon 2 tsp of the anchovy oil over the potatoes. Cover with foil and bake for 30 minutes, then remove the foil and cook for another 20-30 minutes until the top is golden and crisp.

INGREDIENTS

1 medium onion

900g/2lb waxy potatoes

butter, for greasing

15 anchovy fillets

140ml/5fl oz vegetable stock

285ml/10fl oz double cream

freshly ground black pepper

Salmon Pasta Bake

If you don't have any tinned salmon, tuna will do just as well.

Cook the pasta according to the packet instructions. Drain and set aside. Meanwhile, drain the oil from the tins of salmon into a large pan, add the butter and heat to melt it. Gently fry the onion in this for 10 minutes over a medium heat, until softened. Stir in the soup and 300ml/½ pint of the milk. Bring to the boil, stirring, and cook for a minute or two. Flake the salmon into large chunks and add to the sauce with the spinach, nutmeg, lemon juice and salt and pepper. Mix in the pasta. Add the vegetable stock and reheat to boiling point. Pour into an ovenproof dish. Scatter the grated Parmesan over the top. Toast the almonds in a dry frying pan until lightly golden, then scatter over the dish. Preheat the grill to medium and cook until golden and bubbling, making sure that the almonds don't burn.

To prepare: 5 minutes

To cook: 20-25 minutes

INGREDIENTS

330g/12oz pasta

2 x 200g/7oz tins of salmon

30g/1oz butter

1 onion, chopped

1 x 300g/10½oz tin of condensed mushroom soup

300ml/½ pint milk

1 x 400g/14oz tin cooked spinach, drained

1 tsp freshly grated nutmeg

1 tbsp lemon juice

salt and freshly ground black pepper

725ml/5fl oz vegetable stock

110g/4oz freshly grated Parmesan

55g/2oz almonds

SERVES 4

This quick and easy sauce is perfect for jazzing up vanilla ice cream or fresh fruit!

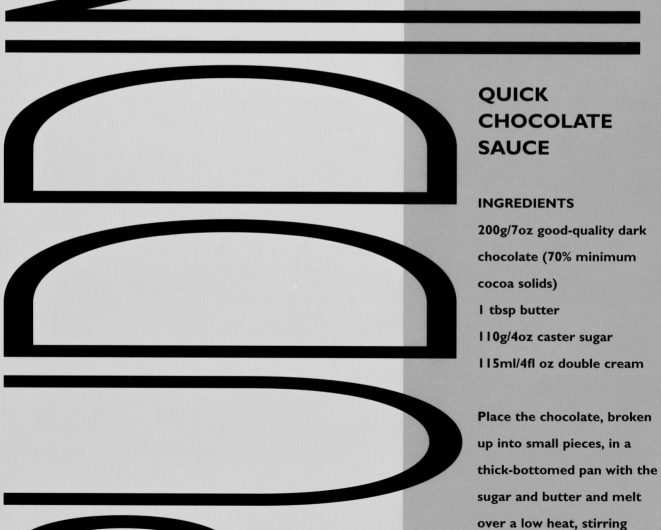

QUICK CHOCOLATE SAUCE

INGREDIENTS

200g/7oz good-quality dark chocolate (70% minimum cocoa solids)

1 tbsp butter

110g/4oz caster sugar

115ml/4fl oz double cream

Place the chocolate, broken up into small pieces, in a thick-bottomed pan with the sugar and butter and melt over a low heat, stirring occasionally. Pour in the cream, still stirring. Serve over ice cream or fruit.

Baked Bananas with Honey

Preheat the oven to 190°C/375°F/gas mark 5. Wrap each peeled banana in kitchen foil leaving the top open. Drizzle the honey over the bananas through the opening, then add 1 tsp of Cointreau, if using, to each foil parcel. Finally, spoon a little orange juice over each one. Close the top of each parcel by scrunching up the foil. Bake in the oven for about 20 minutes or until the bananas are soft. Serve the bananas in their parcels with whipped cream or ice cream.

To prepare: 5 minutes

To cook: 20 minutes

INGREDIENTS

4 ripe bananas, peeled

2 tbsp runny honey

4 tsp Cointreau or orange liqueur (optional)

juice of ½ orange (or 1 tbsp fresh orange juice from a carton)

TO SERVE

whipped cream or ice cream (optional)

To prepare: 35 minutes

To cook: 30 minutes

Bread and Butter Pudding

Try and make this pudding a little in advance to allow soaking time for the bread. If you don't have a full hour to spare, 30 minutes should be enough.

Cut three-quarters of the loaf into medium-thick slices and butter both sides. Cut each slice in half diagonally and layer into a greased oven-proof dish about 8cm/3in deep. Sprinkle with the sultanas. Beat the eggs lightly and add the milk, cream, vanilla essence and caster sugar. Pour carefully over the bread and leave to stand for 1 hour if possible. Heat the oven to 180°C/350°F/gas mark 4. Sprinkle with the demerara sugar and a few more sultanas and place the dish in a roasting tin with warm water to half-way up the dish. Bake for 30 minutes or until just set.

INGREDIENTS

1 small, good-quality white loaf

110g/4oz butter

handful of sultanas

5 medium eggs

570ml/1 pint milk

425ml/15fl oz whipping cream

vanilla essence

55g/2oz caster sugar

3 tbsp demerara sugar

Easy Plum Cake

Serve this hot from the oven with double cream.

Preheat the oven to 180°C/350°F/gas mark 4. Cream the butter and sugar together. Beat the egg lightly and fold into the mixture. Sift the flour, salt and the baking powder and add to the mixture, folding it in it by bit. Add the milk and vanilla essence and cream the mixture together. Pour into a greased dish and distribute the plum halves evenly on the surface. Sprinkle over the brown sugar and the cinnamon and dot with butter. Bake for 30 minutes.

To prepare: 10 minutes

To cook: 30 minutes

INGREDIENTS

55g/2oz butter

110g/4oz caster sugar

1 egg

140g/5oz plain flour

pinch salt

1 tsp baking powder

85ml/3fl oz milk

½ tsp vanilla essence

8 plums, stoned and halved (or about 4 eating apples, peeled and sliced)

55g/2oz brown sugar

1 tsp ground cinnamon

30g/1oz butter, diced

TO SERVE

double cream or ice-cream

Grape Brûlée

You can use all sorts of different soft fruits in this dish.

Halve the grapes. Marinate them in the Cassis for 1 hour if possible. Spoon the fruit and alcohol into a 23cm/9in flameproof flan dish. Whip the cream to stiff peaks and spoon over the fruit. Place in the refrigerator and chill for 30 minutes. Preheat the grill until hot. Sprinkle the sugar over the cream and place under the grill. Watch the brûlée constantly until all the sugar has dissolved evenly, making sure it does not burn. Serve warm or chill until ready to serve.

To prepare: 1-1½ hours

To cook: 5 minutes

INGREDIENTS

450g/1lb green, seedless grapes

2-3 tbsp Cassis or other fruit liqueur

285ml/10fl oz double cream

4 tbsp soft brown sugar

Lemon and Ginger Cheesecake

Place the biscuits between two sheets of greaseproof paper and crush with a rolling pin. Mix together the crumbs and butter and press into the base of a 23cm/9in straight-sided, loose-bottomed flan dish. Chill. Beat the lemon rind, juice, grated ginger, cottage cheese and sugar together. Whisk the condensed milk until thick and then fold in to the mixture. Spread over the biscuit crumbs. Chill for 1 hour.

To prepare: 10 minutes

To chill: 1 hour

INGREDIENTS

170g/6oz ginger nut biscuits

55g/2oz butter, melted

finely grated rind and juice of 2 lemons

15g/½ oz ginger, peeled and finely grated

230g/8oz cottage cheese, sieved

55g/2oz caster sugar

1 small tin condensed milk

Mont Blanc

You can make a slightly lower-fat version of this classic French dessert by using Greek yogurt instead of cream (or try plain low-fat yogurt if you want to be even more virtuous.)

Mix the chestnut purée with the double cream or Greek yogurt, to taste. Vary the quantities according to numbers.

To prepare: 10 minutes

INGREDIENTS

small tin of sweetened chestnut purée

double cream, whipped or

Greek-style yogurt; to taste

Red Berries with Orange Cream

If you use frozen berries, make sure they are thoroughly defrosted. Avoid frozen strawberries if possible.

Divide the berries up between 4 bowls or glasses. Whip the cream until thickened and fold in the icing sugar, vanilla essence and orange zest. Top the glasses with the mixture and decorate each with a sprig of mint.

To prepare: 10 minutes

INGREDIENTS

450g/1lb mixed red berries

425ml/15fl oz whipping cream

1 tsp icing sugar

½ tsp vanilla essence

finely grated zest of 1 orange

fresh mint

Tarte Tatin

Use bought pastry for this recipe.

Peel, core and thinly slice the apples. Preheat the oven to 200°C/400°F/gas mark 6. In a round, shallow, greased gratin dish, layer the butter, sugar and apple slices alternately starting with a thick layer of butter and ending with a layer of apple. Press down well on the apple slices before spreading over the final layer of sugar and butter. Roll out the pastry and cover the dish, trimming off the edges with a knife. Cook for 30 to 40 minutes until the pastry is golden brown. Allow to half-cool. Cover with a large serving plate and turn the dish upside down so that the pastry becomes the base. Carefully lift off the dish and serve warm with cream or Greek yogurt.

To prepare: 5 minutes

To cook: 30-40 minutes

INGREDIENTS

900g/2lb cooking apples

110g/4oz unsalted butter, plus extra for greasing dish

110g/4oz soft brown sugar

230g/8oz puff pastry

butter, for greasing dish

TO SERVE

cream or Greek yogurt

Zabaglione

This is deliciously simple – just make sure you don't overheat it or the egg yolks will curdle. If you don't have Marsala, use sweet sherry or Madeira, or a fruity liqueur.

Place a heat-proof bowl over a pan of barely simmering water so that it fits snugly – alternatively, use a double boiler. Beat the egg yolks in the bowl with the sugar until light and airy and almost white in colour. Add the Marsala. Reduce the heat and beat continuously without allowing the mixture to boil. When the mixture begins to rise, remove from the heat and serve in tall dessert glasses or warmed wine glasses with sponge fingers or other biscuits.

To prepare: 10 minutes

INGREDIENTS

4 egg yolks

75g/2 ½oz caster sugar

130ml/4 ½fl oz Marsala

TO SERVE

sponge fingers or other good biscuits

Index